WOODBURN PUBLIC LIBRARY
280 GARFIELD STREET
WOODBURN, OREGON 97071-4698

Y0-DDR-510

WITHDRAWN

The Wine of Blindness

Poems by

Eden Vale Stevens

The Wine of Blindness

Poems by

Eden Vale Stevens

beMUSEd Press

Shelter Island, New York

Copyright © 2000 by Eden Vale Stevens

Printed in the United States of America

ISBN: 0—615—11520—9

Drawings by Eden Vale Stevens
Critical review by Iris Lee
Design by Jerry Kelly
Printed by BookMasters, Inc.

beMUSEd Press
P. O. Box 1746
Shelter Island, NY 11964-1746

To

Anthony Kiss Stevens

Inspired Teacher

and to

David Fisher and Maxine Rosen

Inspired Friends

When I could no longer deny the life of the spirit, Eden Vale Stevens was there to befriend me and to welcome me into a territory she knew and depicted so well through her paintings, short stories and children's books, and even through the environment she created wherever she happened to be.

Eden was a remarkable guide, perhaps all the more so since she was dealing with a progressive descent into blindness due to macular degeneration.

In recent years, Eden has lived alone, her house nestled in a wooded hollow in Port Orford, a tiny fishing village on the southern Oregon coast. It is an enchanting place that originally had served as an occasional retreat. She had come to know the house in every detail, and to acquire good neighbors like Karim Schumaker and Gayle Wilcox who help her with the tasks she cannot see to do. Under the circumstances, it seemed a safe and secure place to live and create.

It was there that Eden wrote out the poems she was "finding in the darkness." She then sent them to me to be typed and stored in a computer. In this way a body of work gathered, including *In Praise of Praise*, *A Web of Wonder*, *Not Now But Now*, *Fruit of the Tree*, *Life is Singing at the Window*, *Remember?*, *Nightshade*, and the the title poem of this collection.

Recently, I came to know earlier works . . . *Exiled*, *Dance with Me*, *Comfort Me with Love For I am Sick of Apples*, and *The Holy Fool*. Lastly I read the earliest poems including *A Young Recruit* and *An Actress to a Playwright*. Individually and together, the poems had a powerful effect on me and on others who heard and read them.

Through these poems, we are able to hear Eden's voice and admire her courage, her unfailing concern for others, her unwillingness to compromise her values. Despite isolation and cruel deprivation, her intellect, her humanity, her sense of humor remain intact.

I hope I am storing up her example of how to cope—with intelligence, resilience, strength, and perhaps a touch of magic—and to do this while remaining vulnerable and true to what gives life meaning.

In seeking to understand how, under her circumstances, Eden could not only manage the ordinary but create the extraordinary, I have recalled an experience of a few years back. I very much wanted to show

Eden paintings that were important to me. The only way I knew to do so was by reading to her an essay about the works. Her response assured me that she did indeed "see" the paintings: "It doesn't take sight to see, it takes vision."

Although I have known Eden for many years, I know little about her life before we met in the late 1960s. She chooses not to talk about the past. What I have come to know, almost by attrition, has given me glimpses of varied careers in the arts—as a painter, as an actress, and as a writer.

These activities have had considerable public dimension. On the other hand, her poems, while always an important part of her writing, were so personal that she never sent them out for publication. A few of the poems, written over a lifetime of living in the here and now, while simultaneously occupying a space that appears to transcend time and place, are presented in this volume. They are for readers who may want or need to share the ether in which Eden Vale Stevens exists, and from which she offers up her transcendent vision.

Maxine Rosen
Brooklyn Heights, New York

Self portrait
1987

CONTENTS

Italics indicate first line of untitled poems

—————

9

The Wine of Blindness

The Wine of Blindness

The wine of blindness is a bitter wine
Tasting of aloes, thyme and rue.

It stems from an old vine
      rooted in an ailing soil.

The fruit is dark and round on meager clusters.

Gathered by slow old men and peaked children.

Long lain in old caskets
It is very strong.
Drink it slowly in shame and humiliation.

And when the swirling, whirling dervish dance of drunkenness
      upsweeps you, dance and be free.
And when you wake, take stones to weight your clothes
      and walk blindly to the sea.

In Praise of Praise

When time like a beetle ticks in the wainscoting
    Praise the light curving into space denying gravity.

When chaos cracks our order into particles of energy
    Praise Divine Seeing for our being in the Garden.

When our treasures are stolen
    Praise the spaces to be filled.

When we cannot hear
    Praise silence for listening.

If we cannot see
    Praise the dark in which visions like stars sometimes appear.

When only the affluent are invited to the feast
    Praise the homeless for sharing their wealth.

When loneliness lies in a dear companion's place
    Praise sorrow for new ways of knowing.

When a stranger in our land is feared
    And neighbors are no longer speaking
    Praise the heart for breaking.

A Web of Wonder

Into a web of wonder
    wandering
Interstices of ecstasy
     reveal
The stamen of passions
     Vivid
as windsown wildflowers
A field of saffron yellow
Four-petaled flowers
Breathing in the air
     Suddenly
They swirl upward
in the summer air
    swirling
    swirling
A host of amber butterflies
    Then are gone
The field is bare
    wandering
      alone
        wondering

Not Now But Now

The leaves of the year have fallen
One by one.
The last leaf fell into a candle flame
And flew skyward in a plume of smoke.

A new calendar arrives marked to show
Days and hours as currency.
Hurry! Hurry! Hurry!
Time is money.

Animals of ocean, air and land
Are free.
We need time
To go from here to there.

Some know
Now
    is
Where
    we are.

—and I am half in love—

Take away these diamonds
And this gold.
I do not want them
I am old.
My books lie on their shelves unopened
I cannot read them
I am blind.
Birds are singing in the summer trees
I cannot hear them
I am deaf.
Why do I stay?
Keats Byron Shelley—
They lived loved and worked most passionately
His laurels won
Each died
      Fortunately
      young.

Poèt Maudit

Under an unwon sky
He sits on a green bench
Staring at the sea.
An aging man with his father's Cherokee nose
and the mother's Yankee bones.
Staring at the sea.
And the sea is a sea of words
But they are not his words.
His words lie like stones
In the pit of his belly.
Unchosen, wish-whipped
Staring at the sea
Sudden winds shriek his ears
Waves rising usurp the gale.
He sees Whitman's hat tossed high
The venerable beard a sail.
Hears Chaucer's ribald laughter
Old Lear's wails of rage
And the wild swan cries of Yeats.
What should he do in such a company
And his words lying like stones
In the pit of his belly.
He is dying with Keats in a lustre of red blood
With Trelawney kneels to kindle Shelley's heart
And lies with Byron under Italy's sun
Stroking the soft hand of his illicit love.
"I-I-I," he cries. "I-I-I"
And his words lie like stones
In the pit of his belly.

Flowers blooming wild
Or in a glass
Arrange themselves toward light
I, too,—
Might?

Comfort Me with Love for I am Sick of Apples

Passion of roses and firelight
And apples in a silver bowl
Fragrance of rain-drenched roses
And apples in a silver bowl.
Beyond the door the rain
Scent of shadows on wet leaves
And branches heavy with darkness
An old moon is climbing the weary sky.
Passion of roses and firelight
And your place laid at the table
Wine breathes red in two glasses
Passion of firelight
And
    Waiting - - - -

How could I
Displease God
And He
Be
God?

★

Job understood
If God
Were good
We should
Not need
   To Be

A Young Recruit

Are my wing's sinews pliable enough and strong
To sweep aside the contours of my days?
Is this mercurial music singing in my veins
An alchemy of fear or an augury of flight?
I think: the brave are only desperate ones
Who have no corner left in which to cower.
So I shall say goodbye to such as these:
An apple tree,
A fire's glow,
Sunlight on clean white steps.
O, wings, let flight be soon!
If my tears fall—
Let them make dim my eyes—
That I may bear the brightness
Of those silent skies.

*

To feel this sorrow
Is to feel the happiness
I did not know
When I was happy.

Between the Killing Rocks

Who knows what fevers
Rage in the brains
Of Mariners
Who, ears stopped
Against the singing of the Sirens
Imperiled lives and ships
To sail between the Killing Rocks
Scylla and Charybdis
When reaching shore
They find themselves
Unwelcomed
Usurpers
In their own homes.
The downcast eyes
Of wives
Bellies out-burgeoning
With Alien seed
Their sweet mouths
Reshapen
To Another's name
Crying
O! Why
Have you returned
When I have learned
Another
    Way?

Jubilation of Despair

Life is singing at the window
Inside his room
A looking glass
A looking glass
Where naked Peter Lowe
Reflects
Himself.
Clenched fists on pallid stems
Clenched feet on colding floor
Coconut head, round and heavy
On relenting neck.
Eyes
Staring
Eyes
A tide surging
Anxiety surging
There in his looking glass
Clutching clenching rising
Panic
Swelling
Earthfear
Sunfear
Moonfear
Constellating
Shards of light
Squares of black
Sighing seas
Eyes
Eyes
Fathoming
Darkness.
Pinpricks of light
Incise a grid of unborn stars
Pride creating

Peaking shrieking
Jubilation of despair.
Hands fling out
Fling out
Hands fling
Out
Despair.
Life is singing at the window
Singing singing singing
Jubilation of despair
Where
In his looking glass
Looking glass
Looking glass
Peter Lowe
Begins
Begins
   Begins
       to
          Dance . . . .

★

White Moon
Caught in rough embrace
Of Giant Fir
How she struggles
To be free

Trees Stand Watch

Trees stand watch
Rooted in earth's reverence
Sketching seasons
Against the sky.
While we—
Cast out from mystery
Eluding ourselves
Alone as light
Fear-borne
Without wings
Try to fly.

★

Breath shaped on the cold pane
Intrinsic anatomy
Emblazoning
This
Instant

★

On some late beached evening
    of a life
Stopping, maybe, to shake free
    a shoe
of a grain of sand or two,
To watch the sea
    ebb away
obscuring
shall I wonder why?
On some late beached evening
    of a life?

Fortunately I dream
And there are many men and women
And sometimes animals and angels
In my dreams
I sleep long
To find wakening
Very strange—

★

A fool stroking a lion in the darkness is often safer than a God.
However, it is well to remember that lions in a dream may talk,
but in real life they roar.

★

Open your arms without shame
Do not refuse the gift
A broken glass may shine in sunlight
Like jewels
But who can drink from it?

Hummingbird

Fiery jewel
Ablaze with fierce intent
Burning
His piercing beak
Into flowers inmost keep
Iridescent ravager
Insatiable
Implanter
Of loneliness.

Charybdis

Shadows surround me.
Epitome of night—
Let then this moment mean
At least despair.
My only fear is
That I shall not care.

November Dying

Everything I do is a smiling cat-lie
I am listed over like an old tired ship
Mind encrusted impounded in ratrun deaddock
Thick viscous deeppulling mud
Downdrags me into unwary sleep
While rose hymned clouds sail aloft.

Fruit of the Tree

Do not ask the plover flying above
The syntax of our sins
Wind in its wings has no name
The sea below simply is
Stars are
Man has need of words to be
Birds fly.

*

Somewhere, beyond the purpose of the dream
Behind the memory of the night,
Caught like stars in darkness,
Fragrant as flowers dying in the rain,
There is a glimpse of quietude.
No bird sings there—the silence is too sweet.

From requited love we float
Into Nirvana
of
Nothingness
Is it only out of unrequited love
that poems
are
made?

Exodus

Falling seeds
Sharpen serpent tongues
Stabbing his amazed feet
As the eyeless angel
Gazing through open eyes
Stirs his wings' sinews
Divining
Flight

The Marriage

Dawn's burgeoning blossom
Thin-stemmed and frail
Growing in the night
Awaits the Sun.
When Sun and dawn are one
He paints the heavens
With so fiery an abandon
That the whole sky
Is ablaze with Love.

The Holy Fool

The Holy Fool knows
How
The preparation
In Sign of its beginning
Is Fulfilled.

I wish
I wish
I wish

The Holy Fool knows
How
Silently
The Bird
Unscrolls his wings
And as silently
Flies

I wish
I wish
I wish

The Holy Fool knows
How
Sorrows
Heal Slowly
And scorpion Good
Carries a sting
in his tail

I wish
I wish
I wish

———

The Holy Fool knows
How
The Goat-god
Laughs
In the wood
Ravishing
Innocence

I wish
I wish
I wish

The Holy Fool knows
How
I wish
To sing for dear life
From the egg of Then
To
The halcyon raveling
Of
Now.

Who rankles under Time
Has death for Commandant.
Life forages
On Seasons.

Edenweed

June the dappled hound leaps dancing
cold December from her tomb—
All three, you, hound, sweet cold
Come to the open fire:
Sing a weed's song
loving
as the wind loves the weed.

★

Sing then
This rain
Incising
Earth
And Sea
Relentless
As
Unseasoned
    Pain

Exiled

Darkness falls from blackberry fronds
Sullying pond water
Where blind salamanders swim.
Brown leaves foretell the Fall
Even though summer gathers pears in her apron
And cats copulate in thorn beds.
And we—
Who are we
To ask
Why we are
Exiled
Staring down the corridors of Pain
Seeking the Coda
Before we have found the Beginning?

Life is Singing at the Window

Life is singing at the window
We go there—
My heart and eye—
And see
Through the pane
Flowers growing
—And a tree

Do You Remember?

The questing green of tender grass,
Small flowers seeking rain,
Impetuous showers which quickly pass—
A child's tears without pain.
Soft as curry of a furry tribe,
A bird's bright wing.
These are the Spring!
I know Her face since all the winter through
I have known—you.

Remember?

Ducks gobble everything you throw them
Swans float bending their white necks
Seeming too elegant to eat
A small child content in his world
Intently sails his boat
On the path nearby
A gangly girl in jeans skips rope
The lovers hand in hand
Sit beneath the weeping willow tree
She is downcast
He asks her why
She shakes her head
They do not know
Young love is always sad
At last they rise
Leaving the shadows of the tree
To walk together
      Slowly
      Slowly
In the sun
      Suddenly!
They begin to run
        This is a summer's day.

———

37

WOODBURN PUBLIC LIBRARY
WOODBURN, OREGON 97071-4698

A tree and time
Who walks in the winter snow
Singing of Spring
A sword swings through the air
Cutting away sorrow.
Sedately walking
We preserve the past.

Nightshade

Dawn is stealing thru the shadows.
"Hush my love."
The woman holds night close.
"Do not awaken. Stay.
She is false."
He does not answer
Night has gone
Leaving her
  Alone
  Forlorn
  Forsaken
For the dawn.

In the inner cave
In the dark circle
In the black abyss
Here he lies
Only I
Bringing
My
Substance
Only
I
Bringing
My
Life
He is my Father
I am his Mother
We are
Our
Own
Parents

Autumn Garden

You were the tree's roots
Entwining me
And forever was the ripe fruit
In our mouths
Wasps glut now on the rotting falls
And deer eat the roses.

To One Whose Name May Not Be Said

One word
Could stop my pain,
One silence
Fraught with pity
Stem a freshet of regret.
Your hand outstretched without a thought
Of self or gain—guides true.
And I may only love the soul of you.

*

In this garden
Lie
Only wind thrifts
I try
To
Find
One
Whole
Apple

*

It is not enough
To be alone
Gnawing on the bones
Of old loves
Death, that lavish caterer
Has prepared
    A Feast—

Annunciation

Darkness climbs trees
Holding light in their crowns.
Close, one to the other,
Brother and Sister
Wait
Alone in this fierce wood
In dark-encircled house
Praying
The parents
Home.
"Listen—"
"Who
is there?"
Clutching her sins like flowers
For bestowing
Bare feet slow
Then running
To the door
She opens
Seeing Him there
In the light of all beginnings
And the endings
Of her days. . .
Wordless
Offering
And in return
Accepting
The credulous anguish of her joys.
And then
When darkness claims
That unresisting light
"Are they home?" he asks.
"No."
"Who came?"

"An angel."
"Oh?"
"Yes."
And the Sister's affirmation
Pleases
Their faith-infected
Waiting . . . .

The Sacrifice

On that high rock of morning
When three suns in one
Struck
Noon
Who heard the kid's pierced bleating
Or marked its falling
And afterward
Did Isaac lead the frantic mother
Down from her discomforting
To fill his cup?

*

Shall I fling my own bones
Beyond
Abyss
Wagering not one glance
Below
To know
Christ's crossing?

Blood
Red Red Blood
Thorn torn
Shout
                    Crucify
Out
                    Him!
Crucify
Crucify

                    ⋆

Receive this round wafer
Drink the red Wine
Dine upon his Breath's
Dying
Fall—

                    ⋆

Open
For All
Accept the wine
Broken reflections seed shame
Who shall
Then drink?

Foolhardy Flowers

Bronze roses in the autumn sun
Blossom though their summer's done.
Though snow is soon,
And icy winds abjure,
Bronze roses in their ignorance
Remain secure.

November Musings

This deliberate foretelling
Eats the air.
How fiercely penned
Is the past
Beginning.

Go forth into unwon spaces
Afraid only of knowing
Without wisdom.
Fetch me cuttings
From the Tree—
If such
There
Be

Fish

War seeps downward
Silting the ocean bed
Upward they rise
Up up
Into the burning light
Dead

★

Light the unbenign spaces
With oracles
Fling high pennants
Of love
Death is known
Only
To Death.

Catnip
Coriander
Crosses three
Black on a white hill
Airborne seeds
Unpodded
Breathe
Free - - -

Young Girls

Innocence pervades
Them with fevers of lust
Assailed by doubt
The young girls
Run away from home.

*

No silver-hooved apparition
Flies through my dreams
Desire
Lies
Dying
In its imaging

An Actress to a Playwright

Out beyond the stars they stand
A silent host with grave expectant eyes.
Their silver silence lies
The words and images—archetypes
Of all great works to be.

To you then who have listened well,
The murmur comes—a warm insistent breeze
To melt the icy intellect,
To break the spell.

Beauty too long held captive
In mortal minds
Flies free.
The silence shatters into song;
And we
Who wait with outstretched hands
Carry your bright gleanings to the world.

Swine, white and petulant
Root
Anemones
Beneath the leafless Tree.
Who moans now
For the dying Sun?

★

In this thicket of light
He lies
With bared throat
Praying
The terror may
Unglutted
Go

★

I am a stone
Within
A stone.
Somewhere
In the upper air
A screen door
Slams.

On this clear air
Who calls?
Through the leaf-striven arches
Unwilling searcher
The answer swings in a clay daubed nest.

★

There is howling in the night
Shrieks and lamentations
Then when day uprooted from darkness
Is flung upward
And thin root hairs of light thread
Back
Back into darkness
Frantically burrowing
Seeking thrown
Seeds of sleep.

★

Irresponsible ravellings
Of Pain
Bedizen my old Mournings
Once
Again
I waive the threat
Of the laying on of hands

Death, we've played before—
Another round?
Don't grin
This win you lose
I
Choose!

Dance With Me

Come Death. While there is yet Time
For me
To be
In grace.
Come, Death, take my hand
While there is yet Time.
Caress me
Embrace me
In my own Space.
Dance with me
To the Beat
Of angels' hands
Clapping.
Good bye, good bye
As though
They could know
Could possibly know
The meaning.

WOODBURN PUBLIC LIBRARY
280 GARFIELD STREET
WOODBURN, OREGON 97071-4698

WITHDRAWN